Where Is My Egg?

by Wiley Blevins • illustrated by Anna Jones

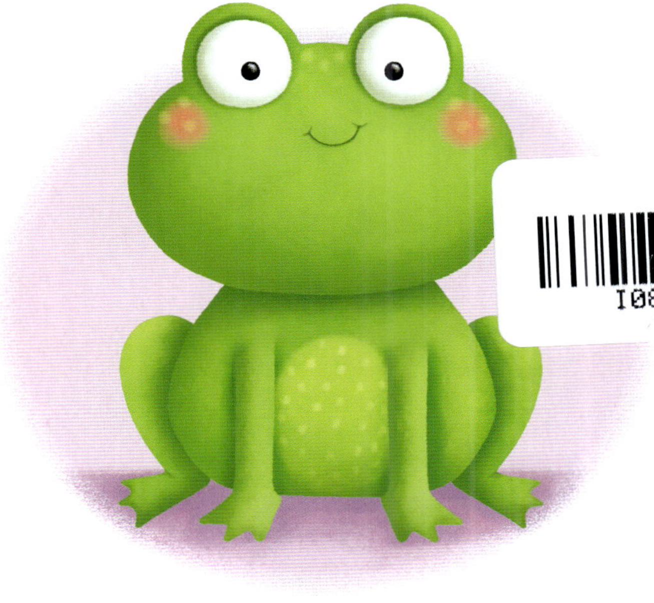

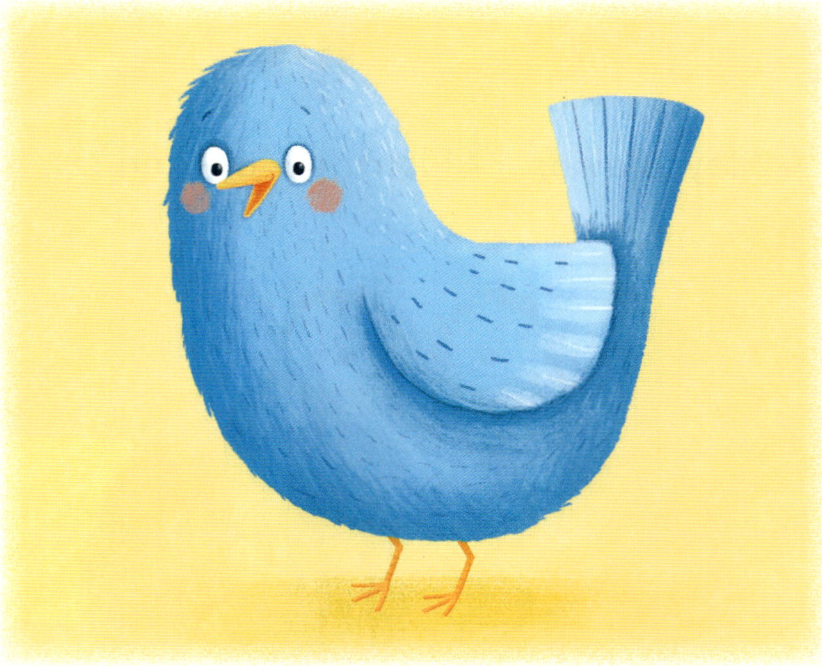

My egg is blue.

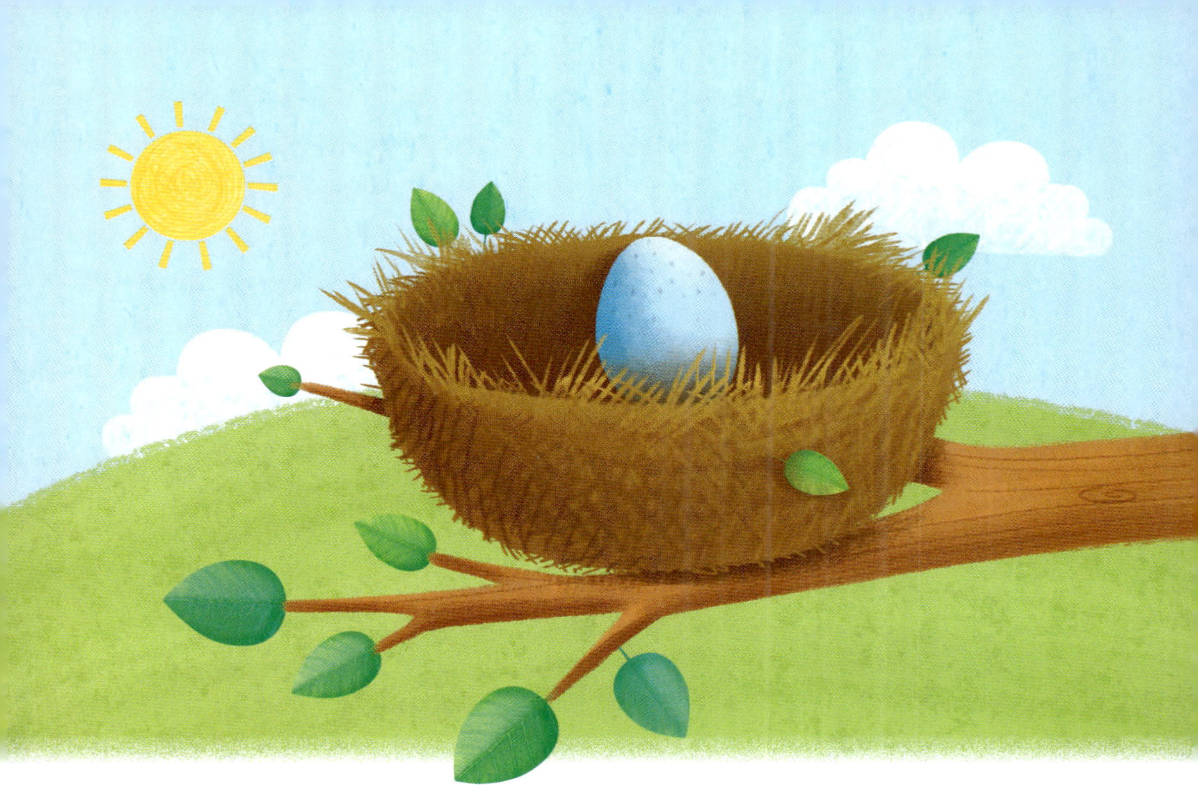

Where is my egg?

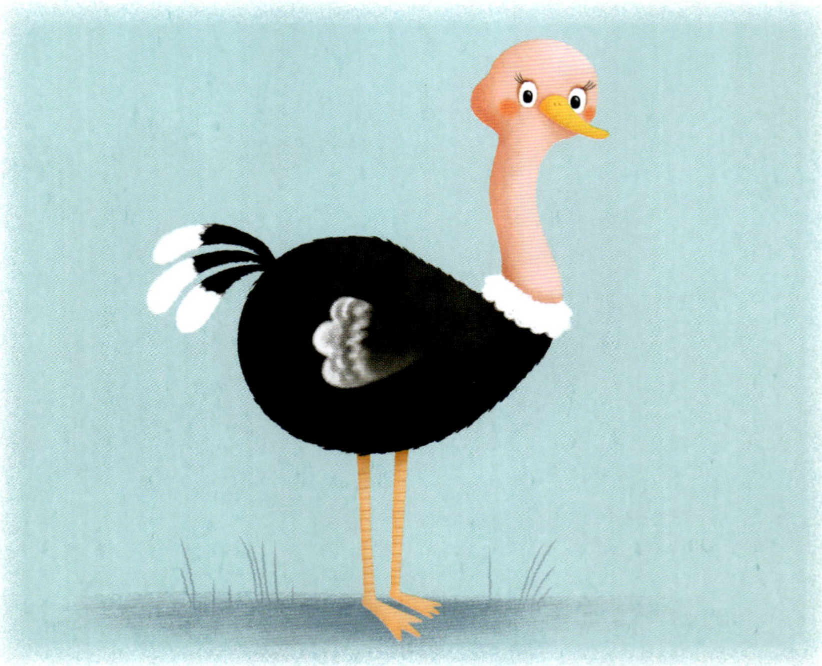

My egg is big.

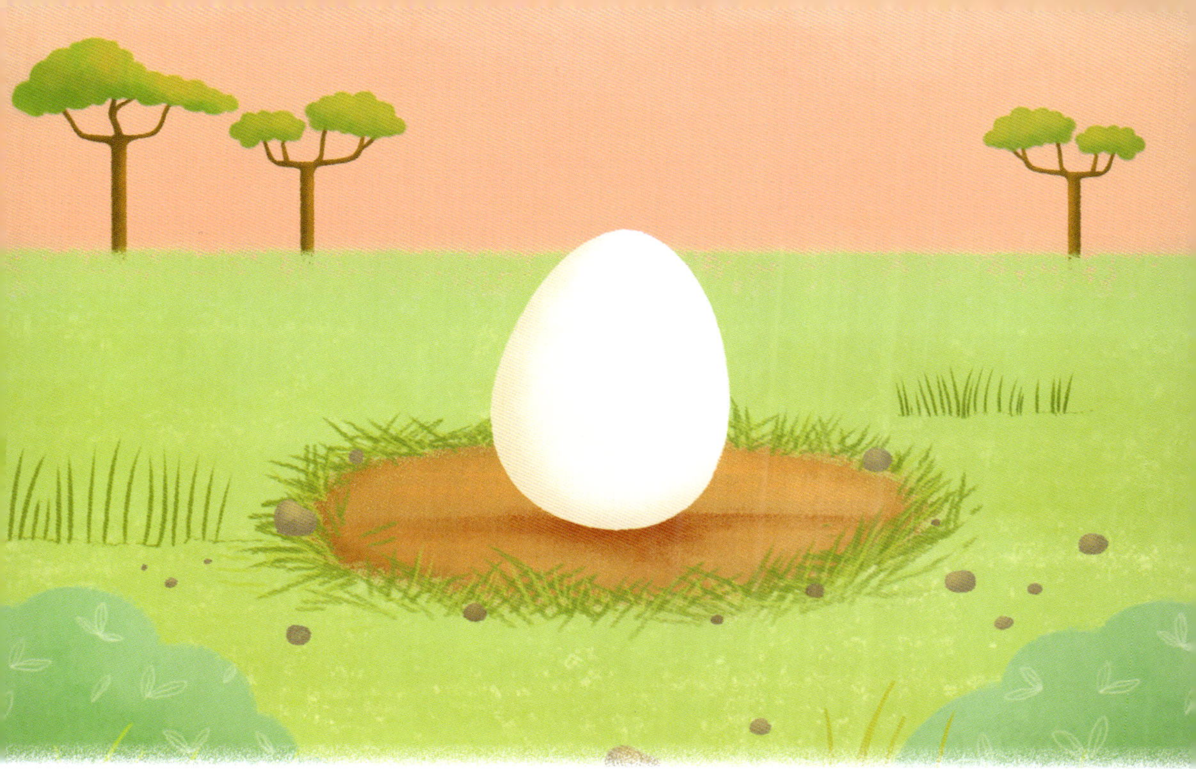

Where is my egg?

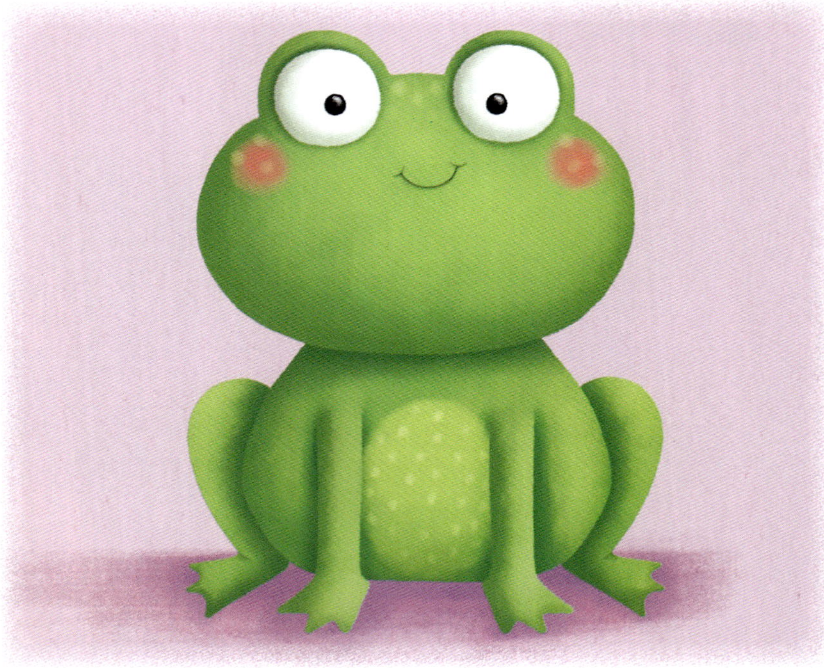

My egg is spotted.

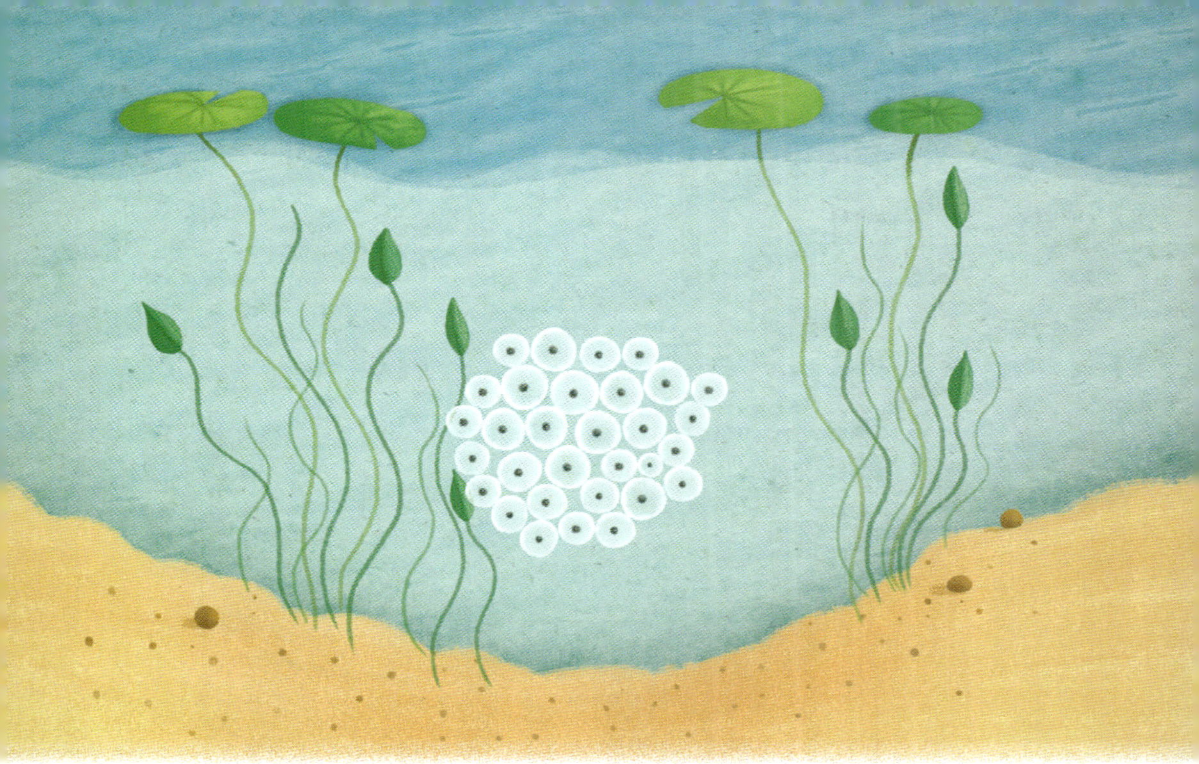

Where is my egg?

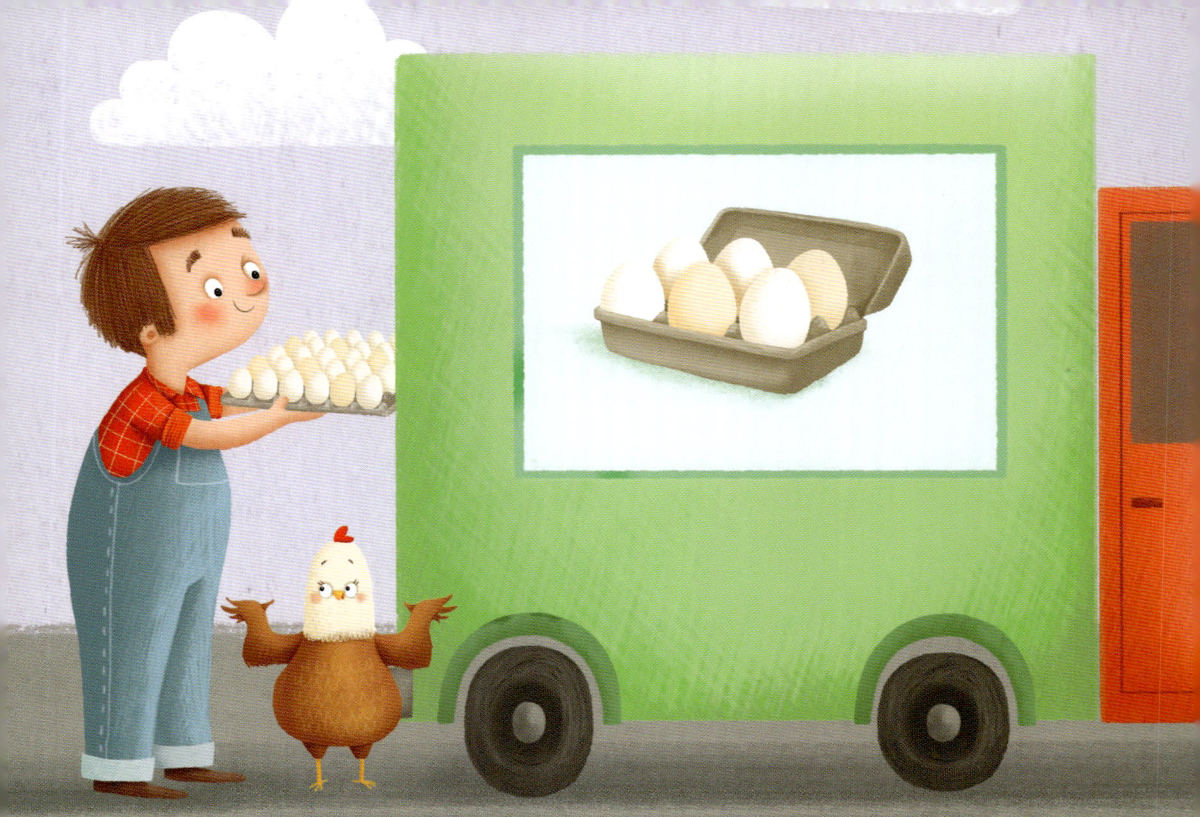

Where is my egg?